Ultimate Listening
無敵リスニング

英語力を伸ばす
ディクトグロスタスク30
30 Dictogloss activities to improve
your English skills

Adrian Leis・Simon Cooke

開拓社

ACKNOWLEDGEMENTS

The authors wish to give special thanks to the following people for their support and advice in putting the Ultimate Listening Series together:

Yuri Kamaya, Kohei Kidachi, Tetsuo Nishihara, Tsugumi Nishoji, Vince Scura, Ryan Spring, Jun Suzuki, and Matthew Wilson.

◆扱う英文を読み上げた音声が、開拓社ホームページからダウンロードできます。
(The audio used for this textbook can be downloaded from the Kaitakusha homepage.)

http://www.kaitakusha.co.jp/book/book.php?c=2311

◆この本には中級編もあります。併せてご利用ください。
(*Ultimate Listening Intermediate* is also available for purchase.)

『無敵リスニング〈中級〉』(Ultimate Listening 〈Intermediate〉)
定価 (Price):本体 1200 円＋税 (¥1200 plus tax)
ISBN978-4-7589-2310-1

Table of Contents

How do you do a dictogloss?   4
Be Active! Discussions to Build Active Learning   6
Improving Your Conversation Skills   7
Dictogloss Progress Chart   8

Stage 1 (75 words)   9
1-1   The Mary River Turtle   10
1-2   Oranges   12
1-3   Rainbows   14
1-4   Cows   16
1-5   The Underwater Waterfall   18

Stage 2 (85 words)   21
2-1   The Seahorse   22
2-2   Honesty and Lying   24
2-3   Polar Bears   26
2-4   How Long is a Jiffy?   28
2-5   Shorthand   30

Stage 3 (95 words)   33
3-1   Strait of Gibraltar   34
3-2   Japanese Carp   36
3-3   Central Park   38
3-4   Salto Hotel   40
3-5   Pluto   42

Stage 4 (105 words)   45
4-1   Cotton Candy   46
4-2   Message in a Bottle   48
4-3   Stamp Collecting   50
4-4   The Immortal Jellyfish   52
4-5   Stock Car Racing   54

Stage 5 (115 words)   57
5-1   City Hall Subway Station   58
5-2   Kaprosuchus Saharicus   60
5-3   Leonardo da Vinci   62
5-4   Green Tea   64
5-5   Snow   66

Stage 6 (125 words)   69
6-1   Professional Video Gamers   70
6-2   Bubble Wrap   72
6-3   The Metric System   74
6-4   Sneezing   76
6-5   Octopuses   78

Passages and Translations   81
List of Vocabulary   91

How do you do a dictogloss?

1. Make a group of two to four people. Read the title of the passage you are going to hear. Discuss with your group members about the topic and what kind of words might appear in the passage. Share anything you know about that topic.
2. Read the first five words of the passage. Try to guess what word, or what kind of word might come next.
3. Discuss and create your strategies for doing the dictogloss with your group members.
4. Listen to the audio. Take memos of words and sentences you hear. The passage will be read quickly, so do not try to write down every word.
5. After listening to the passage once, discuss with your partner (or think alone) about what you heard and try to reconstruct as much of the passage as you can within the time limit. Look at your notes and guess words that might be in the passage.
6. Listen to the passage again and take notes.
7. With your partner, try to reconstruct the passage based on your notes. It's difficult to get 100%, so aim for 70% or higher.
8. Look at the passage (from page 81) and give yourself one point for each word you wrote correctly. Do not give yourself any points for spelling mistakes or wrong words.
9. Calculate your percentage score (the number of words you wrote correctly ÷ the total number of words x 100 (don't include the first five words)) and mark it on the progress chart. e.g., If you write 40 words of the 70 words correctly in level 1-1, you can calculate your percentage as 40 ÷ 70 x 100 = 57%. Numbers nine and under should be written as words, e.g., write nine, not 9. Numbers more than 10 should be written as numbers, e.g., write 10, not ten. These should be counted as one word.
10. Look at the full passage and read the passage silently as you listen to it again.
11. Read the passage aloud. For a challenge, try reading at the same speed as the native speaker.
12. Listen to the passage again without looking at your notes or the passage. Could you catch more this time?
13. Finally, write your reflection. Thinking about your performance in this dictogloss activity, what advice do you have for yourself to do better next time?

Scan the QR Code to watch a video on how to do a dictogloss.

ディクトグロスのやり方

1. 2人～4人のグループを作り、その英文のタイトルから英文の中にどんな話題、どんな英単語が出てくるかを予測し、話し合います。その際、話題について知っていることはなんでも共有しましょう。
2. 最初の5語を読み、6語目にはどんな単語が来るか推測します。
3. グループでディクトグロスの作戦について話し合います。
4. 音声を聞き、聞き取れた単語や文をメモします。読まれるスピードは速いので、文章全部を書こうとする必要はありません。
5. 一度音声を聞いたあと、グループで話し合い、設けられた時間制限の中で、英文をなるべく再現してみましょう。聞き取れなかった単語があっても、自分のメモを見て、どんな語が英文に入るかを推測します。
6. もう一度音声を聞いて、メモをとります。
7. メモをもとに、グループで文章を再現します。100%再現するのは難しいので、70%くらいを目指しましょう。
8. 巻末の英文（81ページ～）と比べてみましょう。自分がメモした単語が正しければ、それぞれに1点を与えます。スペルミスや間違った単語は0点になります。
9. 自分の正解率を計算してProgress Chartに正解率を記入します。（正しく書けた英単語の数÷総単語数×100（総単語数には最初の5個の英単語を含まない。））　例えば、レベル1-1（70語）で40語が正しく書けた場合は40÷70×100 = 57%となります。数字の9以下の一桁の場合は英語のつづりで書きます。例えば、9はnineと書きます。10以上の二桁の数字の場合は数字表記で書きます。つまり、10は10と書いて、Tenとは書きません。これらは一語にカウントされます。
10. 音声をもう一度聞きながら英文を見て黙読します。
11. 今度は、声に出して読みます。できれば、ネイティブスピーカーと同じ速さで読んでみましょう。
12. 自分のメモや英文を見ないでもう一度聞きます。今回は一回目と比べてもっと聞き取れたでしょうか。
13. 最後に自分の意見や感想を書きます。ディクトグロスで自分がどれくらいできたかを考え、次はさらに正解率が上がるように自分なりに改善点を探ってみましょう。

QR Codeをスキャンするとディクトグロスのやり方についてのビデオが見れます。

Be Active! Discussions to Build Active Learning

Active Learning has become a key word in education in recent years. Many teachers and educational institutions use 'Active Learning' as part of the goals for their courses. However, the true definition of Active Learning is not always clear. Some people think that if students are moving around the classroom, they are being active. Others regard pair work as Active Learning. In this book, we use the definition of Active Learning as provided by Grabinger and Dunlap:

> Times have changed. People now need to be able to think flexibly and creatively, solve problems, and make decisions within complex, ill-structured environments.
> (Grabinger & Dunlap, 1995, p. 27)

For us, the keywords in this definition are *flexibly*, *creatively*, *solve problems*, and *make decisions*. At the end of each dictogloss task, we have provided a discussion topic to use in your learning. There is no wrong answer or best answer for these topics. Be flexible and creative in your ideas. As you work through the book, do your best to express your opinions, listen to and respect your classmates' opinions, and think of ways to improve your English.

　近年、教育現場において、アクティブラーニングが注目されています。したがって、授業の目標にアクティブラーニングを設定する先生や教育機関が多くあります。しかし、アクティブラーニングの定義は明らかになっていない場合が多いのです。生徒が教室内を動き回っていれば、それがアクティブラーニングであると思っている人もいれば、生徒がペアワークをやっていれば、それがアクティブラーニングだと思っている人もいます。このテキストでは、グラビンジャーとダンラップという学者が提案したアクティブラーニングの定義を使用します：

> 時代が変わりました。現代の人々は頭を柔らかくし、クリエイティブな考え方を持ち、複雑で不完全な構造の環境で様々な問題を解決し課題について決断を下さなければなりません。　　　　　　(Grabinger & Dunlap, 1995, p. 27)

　本テキストでは、この定義のキーワードを「頭を柔らかくする」、「クリエイティブな考え方」、「問題を解決する」や「決断を下す」とし、各ディクトグロスの最後に、ディスカッションを設けました。間違っている答えや一番良い答えはありません。頭を柔らかくしてクリエイティブな考え方でディスカッションに参加することが大切です。テキストを進める中で遠慮なく自分の意見を述べ、友だちの意見を尊重しながら聞いて、自分の英語力をどう高めるか考えてください。

Improving Your Conversation Skills

How can we improve our conversations and discussions? Here are some tips to help make your conversations and discussions in the Active Learning section go better each time.

1. Try to keep the conversation going.
Rather than giving a simple answer and then passing the question on, try and make your sentence longer. For example, if the question is: 'What is your favorite season?', don't simply say 'I like summer, and you?'.
Instead try to add a comment to your answer before asking the question, like this:
'I like summer. I like summer because I like hot **weather** and I like to eat **ice cream** in summer.'
You see? You now have more topics to talk and ask about – not only summer, but also weather and ice cream!

１．会話を続ける努力をしましょう！
簡単な答えを出して質問を返すのではなく、文章を長くしてみましょう。たとえば、「あなたのお気に入りの季節はどれですか。」という質問がある場合は、単に「私は夏が好きです、あなたは？」と言ってはいけません。
その代わりに、次のように、質問を返す前に、自分の答えにコメントを追加してみてください：
「私は夏が好きです。私は暑い気候が好きなので夏が好きで、そして夏にアイスクリームを食べるのが好きです。」分かりましたか。今の例では話をしたり聞いたりするトピックが増えました。夏だけでなく、天候やアイスクリームも！

2. Give your opinion.
Don't be afraid of giving your opinion on a topic. Giving your opinion can make the conversation more personal.
Try using some of these phrases in your conversation to give an opinion, to agree and disagree and to ask for other people's opinions.

２．自分の意見を伝えましょう！
トピックについて意見を述べることを恐れないで下さい。自分の意見を述べることで、会話をもっと個人的なものにすることができます。あなたの会話でこれらのフレーズのいくつかを使って意見を述べ、同意し、反対し、そして他人の意見を求めましょう。

Giving your opinion 自分の意見を述べる	Agreeing with someone 同意する	Disagreeing with someone 反対する	Asking for other people's opinion 他人の意見を求める
In my opinion,… As for me,… I think… How about this idea?	I agree! That's a great idea! I like your suggestion! I think so, too.	I don't agree,… I'm not sure about that… I have a different opinion. I don't think so.	How about you? What do you think? What ideas do you have? Please share your ideas.

Dictogloss Progress Chart

Color the horizontal bars to record your score.
マスに色を塗り、横の棒線で各タスクのスコア（％）を記録しよう。

Level	Date	0% ~ 9%	10% ~ 19%	20% ~ 29%	30% ~ 39%	40% ~ 49%	50% ~ 59%	60% ~ 69%	70% ~ 79%	80% ~ 89%	90% ~ 100%
1-1											
1-2											
1-3											
1-4											
1-5											
2-1											
2-2											
2-3											
2-4											
2-5											
3-1											
3-2											
3-3											
3-4											
3-5											
4-1											
4-2											
4-3											
4-4											
4-5											
5-1											
5-2											
5-3											
5-4											
5-5											
6-1											
6-2											
6-3											
6-4											
6-5											

Stage 1

Passage: 75 words
Writing time: 3 minutes 30 seconds

1-1 The Mary River Turtle

GET READY

Do you have a pet? What kind of pet would you like to have?

PREDICT

Discuss with a partner and write your predictions.

What do you know about the topic?	What English words do you expect to hear in the story?	What do you think the sixth word will be?
		In Queensland, Australia, there is ...

STRATEGY TIME

What strategies are you going to use this time?

LISTEN

Scan the QR Code to hear the passage. Use this space to take memos as you listen.

RECONSTRUCT

Write the passage here. (Time: 3 minutes 30 seconds)

In Queensland, Australia, there is

(/ 70 = %)

Remember to update your Progress Chart!

REFLECT

How can you do better next time?

ACTIVE LEARNING

Talk with your classmates about the following topics.

- Many people keep turtles as pets. Some people keep more unusual pets. What is the most unusual pet you have heard of someone keeping?

- Imagine you are going to buy a pet at the local pet store. Get some advice regarding the best pet for you and decide what pet you will buy.

1-2 Oranges

GET READY

What kinds of fruits do you like to eat?

PREDICT

Discuss with a partner and write your predictions.

What do you know about the topic?	What English words do you expect to hear in the story?	What do you think the sixth word will be?
		When we hear the word ...

STRATEGY TIME

What strategies are you going to use this time?

LISTEN

Scan the QR Code to hear the passage. Use this space to take memos as you listen.

RECONSTRUCT

Write the passage here. (Time: 3 minutes 30 seconds)

When we hear the word

_____

_____

_____

_____

_____

_____

_____

_____

(/ 70 =   %)

Remember to update your Progress Chart!

REFLECT

How can you do better next time?

ACTIVE LEARNING

Talk with your classmates about the following topics.

- In addition to vegetarians, people who don't eat any meat or fish, some people choose to be fruitarians. These people don't eat anything except fruit and maybe nuts or seeds. Could you be a fruitarian or a vegetarian? Why or why not?

- Research the names of some interesting fruit that you might not find in your own country. Roleplay a conversation of you buying the fruit and asking how to cook it.

1-3 Rainbows

GET READY

Are you superstitious?

PREDICT

Discuss with a partner and write your predictions.

What do you know about the topic?	What English words do you expect to hear in the story?	What do you think the sixth word will be?
		A rainbow is an arc …

STRATEGY TIME

What strategies are you going to use this time?

LISTEN

Scan the QR Code to hear the passage. Use this space to take memos as you listen.

RECONSTRUCT

Write the passage here. (Time: 3 minutes 30 seconds)

A rainbow is an arc

(/70 = %)

Remember to update your Progress Chart!

REFLECT

How can you do better next time?

ACTIVE LEARNING

Talk with your classmates about the following topics.

- What are some things that are considered lucky or unlucky in your country? Do you believe in such superstitions? Why / why not? Rank the top five most popular superstitions on your group.

- Choose one of the superstitions from your list above. Roleplay a conversation between you and an exchange student explaining the importance of that superstition.

1-4 Cows

GET READY

Are you interested in living on a farm?

PREDICT

Discuss with a partner and write your predictions.

What do you know about the topic?	What English words do you expect to hear in the story?	What do you think the sixth word will be?
		Most people like to drink ...

STRATEGY TIME

What strategies are you going to use this time?

LISTEN

Scan the QR Code to hear the passage. Use this space to take memos as you listen.

RECONSTRUCT

Write the passage here. (Time: 3 minutes 30 seconds)

Most people like to drink

_____

_____

_____

_____

_____

_____

_____

_____

(____ / 70 = ____ %)

Remember to update your Progress Chart!

REFLECT

How can you do better next time?

ACTIVE LEARNING

Talk with your classmates about the following topics.

- These days, there are many social networking systems that allow us to keep in contact with friends wherever we go. Do you think social networking systems are a good idea, or are they an invasion of one's privacy?

- Imagine you want to get a cow as a pet. Roleplay a conversation of you trying to persuade your roommate to get a cow as a pet.

1-5 The Underwater Waterfall

GET READY

Where is the most beautiful place you have ever been to?

PREDICT

Discuss with a partner and write your predictions.

What do you know about the topic?	What English words do you expect to hear in the story?	What do you think the sixth word will be?
		Near Mauritius, a country 2000 ...

STRATEGY TIME

What strategies are you going to use this time?

LISTEN

Scan the QR Code to hear the passage. Use this space to take memos as you listen.

RECONSTRUCT

Write the passage here. (Time: 3 minutes 30 seconds)

Near Mauritius, a country 2000

_____

_____

_____

_____

_____

_____

_____

                                                                                                                   (/ 70 =   %)

Remember to update your Progress Chart!

REFLECT

How can you do better next time?

ACTIVE LEARNING

Talk with your classmates about the following topics.

- Many people like to go white-water rafting. Are you interested in rafting and other water sports?

- Look at videos of Niagara Falls and the Maid of the Mist on the Internet. Roleplay a conversation of you buying tickets for you and your friends to ride the Maid of the Mist.

Stage 1 Self Report

How was your progress through Stage 1? Can you do better in Stage 2? Write a few ideas so you'll improve when you attempt the longer passages in Stage 2.

Stage 1 Vocabulary List

Scan the QR Code to practice your vocabulary.

Word	Meaning	Level
according to ~	～による	1-4
appear ~	～に見える	1-3
arc	弧	1-3
coast	海岸	1-5
comfortable	快適	1-4
dew	露	1-3
endangered	絶滅寸前の	1-1
environmental	環境の	1-1
extinct	絶滅した	1-1
faint	（色が）薄い	1-3
fog	霧	1-3
form	形成する	1-3
funky	スタイリッシュな	1-1

Word	Meaning	Level
mist	霧雨	1-3
ocean floor	海底	1-5
optical illusion	目の錯覚	1-5
peel	（果物などの）皮	1-2
protect	守る	1-1
relatively	比較的	1-5
separate	別れる	1-4
similar to ~	～に似る	1-4
snack	軽食	1-2
touch	触る	1-3
turtle	亀	1-1
underwater	水中	1-5

Stage 2

Passage: 85 words
Writing time: 4 minutes

2-1 The Seahorse

GET READY

Do you prefer graceful sports, like ballet, or rougher sports, like mountain bike riding?

PREDICT

Discuss with a partner and write your predictions.

What do you know about the topic?	What English words do you expect to hear in the story?	What do you think the sixth word will be?
		Have you ever seen a ...

STRATEGY TIME

What strategies are you going to use this time?

LISTEN

Scan the QR Code to hear the passage. Use this space to take memos as you listen.

RECONSTRUCT

Write the passage here. (Time: 4 minutes)

Have you ever seen a

(/ 80 = %)

Remember to update your Progress Chart!

REFLECT

How can you do better next time?

ACTIVE LEARNING

Talk with your classmates about the following topics.

- It is most common to see seahorses in aquariums. When did you last visit an aquarium? What did you think were the most beautiful/amazing creatures there?

- Due to overfishing, it is said that the number of fish, especially tuna, is decreasing rapidly. What ideas do you have to solve this problem?

2-2 Honesty and Lying

GET READY

When is it acceptable to tell a lie?

PREDICT

Discuss with a partner and write your predictions.

What do you know about the topic?	What English words do you expect to hear in the story?	What do you think the sixth word will be?
		We often hear the phrase, ...

STRATEGY TIME

What strategies are you going to use this time?

LISTEN

Scan the QR Code to hear the passage. Use this space to take memos as you listen.

RECONSTRUCT

Write the passage here. (Time: 4 minutes)

We often hear the phrase,

_____

_____

_____

_____

_____

_____

_____

(____ / 80 = ____ %)

Remember to update your Progress Chart!

REFLECT

How can you do better next time?

ACTIVE LEARNING

Talk with your classmates about the following topics.

- Is it ever okay to tell a lie? Have you ever told a 'white lie' (a lie that you don't think is so serious)?

- Your partner buys you a shirt for your birthday. However, you don't like it. Roleplay the conversation without hurting your partner's feelings!

2-3 Polar Bears

GET READY

Do you prefer hot or cold? Think about things such as food, drinks, and weather.

PREDICT

Discuss with a partner and write your predictions.

What do you know about the topic?	What English words do you expect to hear in the story?	What do you think the sixth word will be?
		The polar bear is the ...

STRATEGY TIME

What strategies are you going to use this time?

LISTEN

Scan the QR Code to hear the passage. Use this space to take memos as you listen.

RECONSTRUCT

Write the passage here. (Time: 4 minutes)

The polar bear is the

_____

_____

_____

_____

_____

_____

_____

(___ / 80 = ___ %)

Remember to update your Progress Chart!

REFLECT

How can you do better next time?

ACTIVE LEARNING

Talk with your classmates about the following topics.

- Some people keep dangerous animals, such as bears, snakes, and even crocodiles as pets. What do you think about this? Should there be a law that prohibits people from owning such pets?

- Imagine your partner has a polar bear as a pet. You have been asked by the local newspaper to conduct an interview about living with a polar bear. Roleplay the interview.

2-4 How Long is a Jiffy?

GET READY

Are you a last-minute person or do you prefer to be well-prepared?

PREDICT

Discuss with a partner and write your predictions.

What do you know about the topic?	What English words do you expect to hear in the story?	What do you think the sixth word will be?
		If we go out for ...

STRATEGY TIME

What strategies are you going to use this time?

LISTEN

Scan the QR Code to hear the passage. Use this space to take memos as you listen.

RECONSTRUCT

Write the passage here. (Time: 4 minutes)

If we go out for

(/ 80 = %)

Remember to update your Progress Chart!

REFLECT

How can you do better next time?

ACTIVE LEARNING

Talk with your classmates about the following topics.

- The famous Chinese philosopher, Confucius once said: It does not matter how slowly you go so long as you do not stop. What do you think about that? Do you agree?

- You have two assignments that are due in two days. You haven't started either of them! However, your partner has invited you to a party tonight. What will you do? Roleplay the conversation.

2-5 Shorthand

GET READY

Which do you think is more important: nice handwriting or fast typing skills?

PREDICT

Discuss with a partner and write your predictions.

What do you know about the topic?	What English words do you expect to hear in the story?	What do you think the sixth word will be?
		Shorthand is an abbreviated form ...

STRATEGY TIME

What strategies are you going to use this time?

LISTEN

Scan the QR Code to hear the passage. Use this space to take memos as you listen.

RECONSTRUCT

Write the passage here. (Time: 4 minutes)

Shorthand is an abbreviated form

(/80 = %)

Remember to update your Progress Chart!

REFLECT

How can you do better next time?

ACTIVE LEARNING

Talk with your classmates about the following topics.

- Some people say that touch typing (being able to type on a keyboard without looking at the keys) is one of the most important skills for people to learn. What skills do you think everybody should learn before graduating from high school?

- Roleplay a job interview with your partner.

Stage 2 Self Report

How was your progress through Stage 2? Can you do better in Stage 3? Write a few ideas so you'll improve when you attempt the longer passages in Stage 3.

Stage 2 Vocabulary List

Scan the QR Code to practice your vocabulary.

Word	Meaning	Level	Word	Meaning	Level
abbreviated	略されている	2-5	in a jiffy	すぐに	2-4
camouflage	偽装	2-1	measurement	計測	2-4
carnivore	肉食生物	2-3	on end	連続して	2-3
century	100年間	2-4	phrase	ことわざ	2-2
clumsy	不器用な	2-1	polar bear	白熊	2-3
completely	完全に	2-2	policy	方策	2-2
delicate	華奢な	2-1	rapidly	急速に	2-5
describe	細かく説明する	2-4	seahorse	タツノオトシゴ	2-1
fin	ひれ	2-1	shorthand	速記	2-5
fur	柔らかい毛	2-3	snout	突き出た鼻	2-1
global warming	地球温暖化	2-3	steer	（船などを）操る	2-1
habitat	生息地	2-3	substitute	代わりをする	2-5
hide	隠れる	2-3	threaten	脅かす	2-3
hunter	狩人	2-1	well-trained	よく訓練されている	2-5

Stage 3

Passage: 95 words
Writing time: 4 minutes 30 seconds

3-1 Strait of Gibraltar

GET READY

Should we pay higher tax on items made in other countries?

PREDICT

Discuss with a partner and write your predictions.

What do you know about the topic?	What English words do you expect to hear in the story?	What do you think the sixth word will be?
		Between Spain and Morocco, you …

STRATEGY TIME

What strategies are you going to use this time?

LISTEN

Scan the QR Code to hear the passage. Use this space to take memos as you listen.

RECONSTRUCT

Write the passage here. (Time: 4 minutes 30 seconds)

Between Spain and Morocco, you _____

_____

_____

_____

_____

_____

_____

_____

(____ / 90 = ____ %)

Remember to update your Progress Chart!

REFLECT

How can you do better next time?

ACTIVE LEARNING

Talk with your classmates about the following topics.

- Traveling between countries can sometimes be easy, but other times security is very strict. Do you think security should be strict for all people entering your country?

- Communication between people of different backgrounds is essential for international trade to work smoothly. Make a list of the top five important points for international communication in trade to work smoothly.

3-2 Japanese Carp

GET READY

Are young Japanese people losing touch with the traditional Japan?

PREDICT

Discuss with a partner and write your predictions.

What do you know about the topic?	What English words do you expect to hear in the story?	What do you think the sixth word will be?
		The Japanese *koi*, or carp ...

STRATEGY TIME

What strategies are you going to use this time?

LISTEN

Scan the QR Code to hear the passage. Use this space to take memos as you listen.

RECONSTRUCT

Write the passage here. (Time: 4 minutes 30 seconds)

The Japanese *koi*, or carp

(/ 90 = %)

Remember to update your Progress Chart!

REFLECT

How can you do better next time?

ACTIVE LEARNING

Talk with your classmates about the following topics.

- The carp is closely related with Japan. What other animals can you think of that create an image of Japan? Make a list of the top five animals that symbolize Japan.

- Many people like to go on a graduation trip after high school or university. Imagine your group members are going to travel together. Half of you want to travel within Japan and half of you want to travel abroad. Make a decision of where to go.

3-3 Central Park

GET READY

Many schools in Japan have clay school yards. Most schools in western countries have grassed school yards. Which do you think is better: clay or grass?

PREDICT

Discuss with a partner and write your predictions.

What do you know about the topic?	What English words do you expect to hear in the story?	What do you think the sixth word will be?
		One of the most famous ...

STRATEGY TIME

What strategies are you going to use this time?

LISTEN

Scan the QR Code to hear the passage. Use this space to take memos as you listen.

RECONSTRUCT

Write the passage here. (Time: 4 minutes 30 seconds)

One of the most famous

_____

_____

_____

_____

_____

_____

_____

_____

(____ / 90 = ____ %)

Remember to update your Progress Chart!

REFLECT

How can you do better next time?

```
┌─────────────────────────────────────────────────┐
│                                                 │
│                                                 │
│                                                 │
└─────────────────────────────────────────────────┘
```

ACTIVE LEARNING

Talk with your classmates about the following topics.

- Many physical education teachers say young children spend too much time playing computer games and don't get enough exercise. What ideas do you have to increase the amount of time young children play outside?

- Find a map of Central Park on the Internet. Roleplay a conversation of asking for directions around Central Park.

3-4 Salto Hotel

GET READY

Talk about a time you were a little scared.

PREDICT

Discuss with a partner and write your predictions.

What do you know about the topic?	What English words do you expect to hear in the story?	What do you think the sixth word will be?
		Tequendama Falls in Colombia has ...

STRATEGY TIME

What strategies are you going to use this time?

LISTEN

Scan the QR Code to hear the passage. Use this space to take memos as you listen.

RECONSTRUCT

Write the passage here. (Time: 4 minutes 30 seconds)

Tequendama Falls in Colombia has _____

_____

_____

_____

_____

_____

_____

_____

(/ 90 =   %)

Remember to update your Progress Chart!

REFLECT

How can you do better next time?

ACTIVE LEARNING

Talk with your classmates about the following topics.

- Salto Hotel has a reputation of being haunted. Do you think you could stay in a haunted hotel? How much money would you have to be paid in order to be convinced to stay in a haunted hotel?

- You made a booking to stay at an expensive hotel. You booked a non-smoking room, but when you went to the room, it smelled like cigarettes. Roleplay a conversation between you and the person working at the front desk of the hotel.

3-5 Pluto

GET READY

Are you more interested in traveling to space or in exploring the oceans on Earth?

PREDICT

Discuss with a partner and write your predictions.

What do you know about the topic?	What English words do you expect to hear in the story?	What do you think the sixth word will be?
		Pluto was discovered in 1930 ...

STRATEGY TIME

What strategies are you going to use this time?

LISTEN

Scan the QR Code to hear the passage. Use this space to take memos as you listen.

RECONSTRUCT

Write the passage here. (Time: 4 minutes 30 seconds)

Pluto was discovered in 1930

(/90 = %)

Remember to update your Progress Chart!

REFLECT

How can you do better next time?

ACTIVE LEARNING

Talk with your classmates about the following topics.

- A lot of money is spent on searching for intelligent life on other planets. Some people say this is a waste of money, whereas others say we need to spend more. What do you think? Should we spend more money to explore space?

- Imagine you have been asked to interview the first human to visit Pluto. Roleplay the conversation.

Stage 3 Self Report

How was your progress through Stage 3? Can you do better in Stage 4? Write a few ideas so you'll improve when you attempt the longer passages in Stage 4.

Stage 3 Vocabulary List

Scan the QR Code to practice your vocabulary.

Word	Meaning	Level	Word	Meaning	Level
accommodate	泊めることができる	3-4	hit hard times	苦しい状況になる	3-4
adorn with ~	～で装飾する	3-3	keep as a pet	ペットとして飼う	3-2
billion	10億	3-3	Neptune	海王星	3-5
breathtaking	息をのむような	3-4	noticeable by ~	～で分かる	3-2
cargo ship	貨物船	3-1	planet	惑星	3-5
carp	鯉	3-2	Pluto	冥王星	3-5
cliff	崖	3-4	propose	提案する	3-1
[be] considered ~	～だと思われる	3-5	provide	与える	3-4
consume	食べる	3-2	reality	現実	3-1
contaminate	汚染する	3-4	reclassify	再分類する	3-5
diameter	直径	3-5	regular	定期的な	3-1
discover	発見する	3-5	solar system	太陽系	3-5
dwarf planet	準惑星	3-5	spooky	不気味な	3-4
engineer	技術者	3-1	strait	海峡	3-1
eventually	結局	3-4	unfortunately	残念ながら	3-4
goldfish	金魚	3-2			
[be] haunted	～には幽霊が出る	3-4			

Stage 4

Passage: 105 words
Writing time: 5 minutes

4-1 Cotton Candy

GET READY

Do you prefer sweet food or salty food?

PREDICT

Discuss with a partner and write your predictions.

What do you know about the topic?	What English words do you expect to hear in the story?	What do you think the sixth word will be?
		At many festivals around the ...

STRATEGY TIME

What strategies are you going to use this time?

LISTEN

Scan the QR Code to hear the passage. Use this space to take memos as you listen.

RECONSTRUCT

Write the passage here. (Time: 5 minutes)

At many festivals around the _____

_____

_____

_____

_____

_____

_____

_____

(____ / 100 = ____ %)

Remember to update your Progress Chart!

REFLECT

How can you do better next time?

ACTIVE LEARNING

Talk with your classmates about the following topics.

- Because it is made from sugar, cotton candy is not very healthy. However, most of us tend to eat some unhealthy food from time to time. What are your three favorite unhealthy foods?

- Imagine you have been asked to interview Japanese students about healthy eating. Roleplay the interview.

4-2 Message in a Bottle

GET READY

What would you do if you found a bottle with a message in it at the beach?

PREDICT

Discuss with a partner and write your predictions.

What do you know about the topic?	What English words do you expect to hear in the story?	What do you think the sixth word will be?
		When we write messages, we ...

STRATEGY TIME

What strategies are you going to use this time?

LISTEN

Scan the QR Code to hear the passage. Use this space to take memos as you listen.

RECONSTRUCT

Write the passage here. (Time: 5 minutes)

When we write messages, we

_____

_____

_____

_____

_____

_____

_____

(____ / 100 = ____ %)

Remember to update your Progress Chart!

REFLECT

How can you do better next time?

ACTIVE LEARNING

Talk with your classmates about the following topics.

- Some people say that 'the art of letter writing is dying.' Do you agree? When did you last write a letter to someone? Do you prefer to use your phone or computer to write? Why?

- Imagine you find a cell phone near the station. Roleplay a conversation handing in the phone at Lost and Found.

4-3 Stamp Collecting

GET READY

Do you have a hobby?

PREDICT

Discuss with a partner and write your predictions.

What do you know about the topic?	What English words do you expect to hear in the story?	What do you think the sixth word will be?
		People have been collecting stamps ...

STRATEGY TIME

What strategies are you going to use this time?

LISTEN

Scan the QR Code to hear the passage. Use this space to take memos as you listen.

RECONSTRUCT

Write the passage here. (Time: 5 minutes)

People have been collecting stamps

(/ 100 = %)

Remember to update your Progress Chart!

REFLECT

How can you do better next time?

ACTIVE LEARNING

Talk with your classmates about the following topics.

- Collecting things, such as stamps, baseball cards, and coins, is a very popular hobby. Have you ever collected anything? Why do you think this is such a popular hobby? Share your thoughts with some classmates.

- Imagine you are sending a box of clothes back to Japan after living abroad for a year. Roleplay the conversation at the post office.

4-4 The Immortal Jellyfish

GET READY

Do you like to eat seafood? What is your favorite way to eat seafood?

PREDICT

Discuss with a partner and write your predictions.

What do you know about the topic?	What English words do you expect to hear in the story?	What do you think the sixth word will be?
		The average life expectancy for ...

STRATEGY TIME

What strategies are you going to use this time?

LISTEN

Scan the QR Code to hear the passage. Use this space to take memos as you listen.

RECONSTRUCT

Write the passage here. (Time: 5 minutes)

The average life expectancy for _____

_____

_____

_____

_____

_____

_____

(_____ / 100 = _____ %)

Remember to update your Progress Chart!

REFLECT

How can you do better next time?

ACTIVE LEARNING

Talk with your classmates about the following topics.

- Immortality and the search for the 'Holy Grail' have been topics for fiction writers for many years. Would you like to live forever? What are the good/bad points of immortality?

- The immortality of the jellyfish is like having a superpower. What superpower would you like to have? In your group, rank the top five superpowers you want.

4-5 Stock Car Racing

GET READY

Do you think high school students should be allowed to drive? What is an appropriate age for someone to learn to drive?

PREDICT

Discuss with a partner and write your predictions.

What do you know about the topic?	What English words do you expect to hear in the story?	What do you think the sixth word will be?
		Stock car racing is a ...

STRATEGY TIME

What strategies are you going to use this time?

LISTEN

Scan the QR Code to hear the passage. Use this space to take memos as you listen.

RECONSTRUCT

Write the passage here. (Time: 5 minutes)

Stock car racing is a

(/ 100 = %)

Remember to update your Progress Chart!

REFLECT

How can you do better next time?

ACTIVE LEARNING

Talk with your classmates about the following topics.

- Extreme sports, such as white water kayaking and cave diving, are sports that are seen by most people as dangerous. However, those who participate in them say they can't get enough. Are you interested in such sports? Why or why not?

- Imagine you have been asked by the local radio to interview a Formula One driver about tips to be a safe driver. Roleplay the interview.

Stage 4 Self Report

How was your progress through Stage 4? Can you do better in Stage 5? Write a few ideas so you'll improve when you attempt the longer passages in Stage 5.

Stage 4 Vocabulary List

Scan the QR Code to practice your vocabulary.

Word	Meaning	Level
achieve	達成する	4-4
at least	少なくとも	4-4
cotton candy	綿あめ	4-1
dentist	歯医者	4-1
deserted island	無人島	4-2
engine	エンジン	4-5
examine	調べる	4-4
fine	細い	4-1
fluffy	ふわふわしている	4-1
funnel	じょうご	4-1
immediate	すぐの	4-2
immortal	不死の	4-4
in theory	理論的に	4-4
invent	発明する	4-1
jellyfish	クラゲ	4-4

Word	Meaning	Level
life expectancy	寿命	4-4
look similar to ~	～に似る	4-5
melt	溶かす	4-1
ocean	大洋	4-2
once again	もう一度	4-4
oval	楕円形の	4-5
part	部品	4-5
rarity	珍しさ	4-3
stamp	切手	4-3
stick	棒	4-1
stock car	改造車	4-5
thread	糸	4-1
tropical region	熱帯地域	4-4
value	価値	4-3

Stage 5

Passage: 115 words
Writing time: 5 minutes

5-1 City Hall Subway Station

GET READY

Do you prefer to catch the bus or the train?

PREDICT

Discuss with a partner and write your predictions.

What do you know about the topic?	What English words do you expect to hear in the story?	What do you think the sixth word will be?
		New York City is full ...

STRATEGY TIME

What strategies are you going to use this time?

LISTEN

Scan the QR Code to hear the passage. Use this space to take memos as you listen.

RECONSTRUCT

Write the passage here. (Time: 5 minutes)

New York City is full

(_____ / 110 = ____ %)

Remember to update your Progress Chart!

REFLECT

How can you do better next time?

ACTIVE LEARNING

Talk with your classmates about the following topics.

- Do you think old city buildings need to be protected or should we keep developing and creating new buildings to replace them when they get old? How do you think technology can make living and working spaces more comfortable and environmentally friendly?

- Although City Hall Subway Station is no longer used, you might still be able to see it if you join a tour. Find a tour on the Internet and roleplay a conversation in which you wish to join one of the tours you find.

5-2 Kaprosuchus Saharicus

GET READY

Is it important to study about dinosaurs and other creatures that lived millions of years ago?

PREDICT

Discuss with a partner and write your predictions.

What do you know about the topic?	What English words do you expect to hear in the story?	What do you think the sixth word will be?
		Paleontologists are people who study ...

STRATEGY TIME

What strategies are you going to use this time?

LISTEN

Scan the QR Code to hear the passage. Use this space to take memos as you listen.

RECONSTRUCT

Write the passage here. (Time: 5 minutes)

Paleontologists are people who study

_____

(___ / 110 = ___ %)

Remember to update your Progress Chart!

REFLECT

How can you do better next time?

ACTIVE LEARNING

Talk with your classmates about the following topics.

- Many children are interested in dinosaurs. How about you? What were you most interested in when you were a child?

- Some movies are based on stories about scientists using DNA to bring dinosaurs back to life. Do you agree with scientists using DNA to resurrect animals that are extinct? Have a debate in your groups, with half agreeing and half disagreeing.

5-3 Leonardo da Vinci

GET READY

Who is your favorite person in history?

PREDICT

Discuss with a partner and write your predictions.

What do you know about the topic?	What English words do you expect to hear in the story?	What do you think the sixth word will be?
		Leonardo da Vinci was a ...

STRATEGY TIME

What strategies are you going to use this time?

LISTEN

Scan the QR Code to hear the passage. Use this space to take memos as you listen.

RECONSTRUCT

Write the passage here. (Time: 5 minutes)

Leonardo da Vinci was a

_____

(____ / 110 = ____ %)

Remember to update your Progress Chart!

REFLECT

How can you do better next time?

ACTIVE LEARNING

Talk with your classmates about the following topics.

- Leonardo da Vinci was part of a small percent of the population who are ambidextrous. Do you think ambidexterity is a skill from birth, or do you think you could train yourself to be ambidextrous?

- You can find examples of art work and inventions by Leonardo da Vinci on the Internet. Find some examples, choose one and roleplay an interview with Leonardo da Vinci about his thoughts while creating that work.

5-4 Green Tea

GET READY

Do you prefer green tea or coffee?

PREDICT

Discuss with a partner and write your predictions.

What do you know about the topic?	What English words do you expect to hear in the story?	What do you think the sixth word will be?
		Although many people tend to ...

STRATEGY TIME

What strategies are you going to use this time?

LISTEN

Scan the QR Code to hear the passage. Use this space to take memos as you listen.

RECONSTRUCT

Write the passage here. (Time: 5 minutes)

Although many people tend to

(/110 = %)

Remember to update your Progress Chart!

REFLECT

How can you do better next time?

ACTIVE LEARNING

Talk with your classmates about the following topics.

- Green tea is used in a variety of cooking. Make a menu for a restaurant that has green tea in everything on the menu. Make sure you have some variety and include at least three entrées, main dishes, desserts, and drinks on your menu. Finally, give your restaurant a name.

- Your friend from abroad is about to participate in a tea ceremony for the first time. Roleplay a conversation with your friend explaining how the ceremony is conducted.

5-5 Snow

GET READY

What do you like to do in winter?

PREDICT

Discuss with a partner and write your predictions.

What do you know about the topic?	What English words do you expect to hear in the story?	What do you think the sixth word will be?
		American singer Bing Crosby once …

STRATEGY TIME

What strategies are you going to use this time?

LISTEN

Scan the QR Code to hear the passage. Use this space to take memos as you listen.

RECONSTRUCT

Write the passage here. (Time: 5 minutes)

American singer Bing Crosby once

_____

(___ / 110 = ___ %)

Remember to update your Progress Chart!

REFLECT

How can you do better next time?

ACTIVE LEARNING

Talk with your classmates about the following topics.

- Snow opens up a wide range of possible sports and activities, such as snowboarding, tobogganing, and snow fights. With a partner, write a list of the five most fun activities you do (or would like to do) when it snows.

- You have decided to go skiing for a week in France. You need to rent equipment and clothing. Roleplay a conversation at the ski resort to rent what you will need.

Stage 5 Self Report

How was your progress through Stage 5? Can you do better in Stage 6? Write a few ideas so you'll improve when you attempt the longer passages in Stage 6.

Stage 5 Vocabulary List

Scan the QR Code to practice your vocabulary.

Word	Meaning	Level	Word	Meaning	Level
absorb	吸収する	5-5	immensely	非常に	5-3
armored	装甲を施した	5-3	intake	摂取	5-4
associate [A] with [B]	[A]といえば[B]を思い出す	5-4	jolt	活力	5-4
at the same time	同時に	5-3	monk	僧	5-4
brass	真ちゅうの	5-1	obviously	明らかに	5-5
caffeine	カフェイン	5-4	originate in ~	～で始まる	5-4
complex	複雑な	5-5	paleontologist	古生物学者	5-2
creature	生き物	5-2	preserve	保存する	5-2
crescent	三日月	5-3	sculptor	彫刻家	5-3
crystal	結晶	5-5	sharp curve	急カーブ	5-1
dagger	短剣	5-2	skeleton	骨格	5-2
dimly	ぼんやりと	5-3	skull	頭骸骨	5-2
dinosaur	恐竜	5-2	skylight	天窓	5-1
entire	全ての	5-1	snowshoe	かんじき	5-3
exist	存在する	5-2	structure	構造	5-5
fixture	設備	5-1	trillion	一兆	5-5
float	浮かぶ	5-3	tusk	牙	5-2
historian	歴史家	5-4	vapor	蒸気	5-5

Stage 6

Passage: 125 words
Writing time: 5 minutes

6-1 Professional Video Gamers

GET READY

Describe your ideal work lifestyle and routine.

PREDICT

Discuss with a partner and write your predictions.

What do you know about the topic?	What English words do you expect to hear in the story?	What do you think the sixth word will be?
		For many people, playing video ...

STRATEGY TIME

What strategies are you going to use this time?

LISTEN

Scan the QR Code to hear the passage. Use this space to take memos as you listen.

RECONSTRUCT

Write the passage here. (Time: 5 minutes)

For many people, playing video

(/ 120 = %)

Remember to update your Progress Chart!

REFLECT

How can you do better next time?

ACTIVE LEARNING

Talk with your classmates about the following topics.

- The number of children who play video games is increasing. However, some children play games too much. In your opinion, how long should elementary school children be allowed to play video games each day? Recommend a number for weekdays and weekends.

- Imagine you have just arrived in a foreign country, planning to stay for a year. You are at a shop buying a cell phone. Roleplay the conversation.

6-2 Bubble Wrap

GET READY

Bubble wrap is often used to protect items that are important for us. What are some items that are important for you that need protection?

PREDICT

Discuss with a partner and write your predictions.

What do you know about the topic?	What English words do you expect to hear in the story?	What do you think the sixth word will be?
		If you ever need to ...

STRATEGY TIME

What strategies are you going to use this time?

LISTEN

Scan the QR Code to hear the passage. Use this space to take memos as you listen.

RECONSTRUCT

Write the passage here. (Time: 5 minutes)

If you ever need to

_____

(____ / 120 = ____ %)

Remember to update your Progress Chart!

REFLECT

How can you do better next time?

ACTIVE LEARNING

Talk with your classmates about the following topics.

- Most people feel some kind of stress from time to time. Some people like to pop the bubbles on bubble wrap and say it relieves stress. How do you relieve your stress?

- You are at the airport getting ready to travel abroad. You have some fragile objects in your suitcase and want to make sure they will be safe in the plane during the flight. Roleplay the conversation with the ticket clerk.

6-3 The Metric System

GET READY

In English, there is a phrase, "to go the distance," which means to be persistent until the end of a task. Tell a story about a time you "went the distance."

PREDICT

Discuss with a partner and write your predictions.

What do you know about the topic?	What English words do you expect to hear in the story?	What do you think the sixth word will be?
		The Metric System is a ...

STRATEGY TIME

What strategies are you going to use this time?

LISTEN

Scan the QR Code to hear the passage. Use this space to take memos as you listen.

RECONSTRUCT

Write the passage here. (Time: 5 minutes)

The Metric System is a

(/ 120 = %)

Remember to update your Progress Chart!

REFLECT

How can you do better next time?

ACTIVE LEARNING

Talk with your classmates about the following topics.

- Although most countries have adopted the Metric System, the majority still use their own currency. Do you think more countries should adopt the same currency such as we see in Europe? Why or why not?

- You are discussing building a shopping center in your town with a builder from abroad, but you use the Metric System and the builder uses the traditional measurements. Roleplay the conversation. (You can find a Metric System conversation chart on the Internet to help you.)

6-4 Sneezing

GET READY

What do you do in order not to catch a cold? Do you have any secrets to keep healthy?

PREDICT

Discuss with a partner and write your predictions.

What do you know about the topic?	What English words do you expect to hear in the story?	What do you think the sixth word will be?
		If I were to have ...

STRATEGY TIME

What strategies are you going to use this time?

LISTEN

Scan the QR Code to hear the passage. Use this space to take memos as you listen.

RECONSTRUCT

Write the passage here. (Time: 5 minutes)

If I were to have

(____ / 120 = ____ %)

Remember to update your Progress Chart!

REFLECT

How can you do better next time?

ACTIVE LEARNING

Talk with your classmates about the following topics.

- Sometimes, a sneeze can be very loud. This can be embarrassing for the person who sneezes or annoying for people around that person, especially during an exam. Do you try to hold in your sneeze? If yes, how? If no, why not?

- Imagine you have caught a cold and are at the drug store buying some medicine. Roleplay the conversation with the store clerk. Remember to talk about the symptoms of your cold.

6-5 Octopuses

GET READY

Octopuses are able to change shape and color to easily hide. Tell a story about a time you wished you could change shape and color to easily hide.

PREDICT

Discuss with a partner and write your predictions.

What do you know about the topic?	What English words do you expect to hear in the story?	What do you think the sixth word will be?
		It is generally agreed upon ...

STRATEGY TIME

What strategies are you going to use this time?

LISTEN

Scan the QR Code to hear the passage. Use this space to take memos as you listen.

RECONSTRUCT

Write the passage here. (Time: 5 minutes)

It is generally agreed upon

(____ / 120 = ____ %)

Remember to update your Progress Chart!

REFLECT

How can you do better next time?

ACTIVE LEARNING

Talk with your classmates about the following topics.

- Octopuses have eight limbs. Although humans don't need eight arms, sometimes, it would be convenient to have one more. If humans had a third arm, where do you think it should be?

- There are many famous fish markets around the world, such as in Seattle, Madrid, and, of course, Tokyo. Roleplay a conversation at a fish market. You need to buy at least five different varieties of seafood. Think about how much you need (weight) and be sure to check the price for each item.

Stage 6 Self Report

How was your progress through Stage 6? Did you feel your listening skills improved throughout this book? What listening strategies did you learn?

Stage 6 Vocabulary List

Scan the QR Code to practice your vocabulary.

Word	Meaning	Level
a good chance	可能性が高い	6-4
bacteria	細菌	6-4
breakable	壊れやすい	6-2
bubble wrap	気泡シート	6-2
bump	ぶつける	6-2
camouflage	偽装	6-5
cushion	衝撃などをやわらげるもの	6-2
deadly	命に関わる	6-5
deter	妨げる	6-2
equivalent	同等のもの	6-3
escape	逃げる	6-5
essential	欠くことができない	6-2
honor	名誉	6-1
human	人間	6-4
hunt	狩る	6-5
inch	インチ（2.54センチメートル）	6-3
intelligent	賢い	6-5
measurement	測定法	6-3

Word	Meaning	Level
metric system	メートル法	6-3
mimic	擬態する	6-5
pepper	コショウ	6-4
pinch	つまむ	6-4
pound	ポンド（453グラム）	6-3
quantity	数量	6-3
reaction	反応	6-4
research	研究	6-4
rib	肋骨	6-4
rupture	破裂する	6-4
sneeze	くしゃみ	6-4
sponsor	提供者	6-1
vein	血管	6-4
venomous	有毒な	6-5
video arcade	ゲームセンター	6-1
virus	ウイルス	6-4
wallpaper	壁紙	6-2
yard	ヤード（91センチメートル）	6-3

Passages and Translations

1-1 The Mary River Turtle （カクレガメ）
In Queensland, Australia, there is a river called the Mary River. There are many unusual animals living in this river, one of which is the Mary River Turtle. One of the first things you'll notice about this turtle is that it seems to have funky hair. Although they were very popular as pets in the 1960s and 1970s, they are now endangered, so many environmental groups are working to protect this animal from becoming extinct.
オーストラリアのクイーンズランド州に、マレー川という川がある。この川にはたくさんの珍しい動物が生息しており、その一つがカクレガメである。このカメについて最初に気づくことは、このカメがスタイリッシュな髪型をしていることだ。１９６０年代から１９７０年代にかけてペットとして非常に人気があったが、今では絶滅危惧種で、多くの環境保護団体がこの動物を絶滅の危機から守ろうと活動している。

1-2 Oranges （オレンジ）
When we hear the word orange, we often think of either the color or the fruit. Maybe you think of both. In fact, the fruit was first, and the color was named after the fruit. Oranges can be eaten raw, made into a juice, or you can use the peel to add a nice smell in cooking. There are many varieties of oranges, most of which are full of vitamins, making them the perfect snack.
オレンジという言葉を聞いて、私たちはよく、色もしくは果物を思い浮かべる。どちらも思い浮かべるかもしれない。実は、果物が最初で、その果物から色の名前が付けられたのだ。オレンジは生でそのままで食べたり、ジュースにしたり、そして香りづけに皮を料理の際に使ったりもする。様々な種類のオレンジがあり、ビタミンが豊富であるためおやつには最適だ。

1-3 Rainbows （虹）
A rainbow is an arc with seven colors that forms in the sky. Rainbows are, in fact, full circles, but because we usually see them from the ground, they appear to be semi-circles. You can see rainbows not only in rain, but also in fog, mist, and dew. If you are lucky, you might see a double rainbow, with one clear rainbow and one fainter arc. However, you'll never be able to actually touch one.
虹は空に形成される７色の弧である。虹は実際には真ん丸の輪の形であるが、いつも地上から見るため半円に見えるのだ。虹が見られるのは雨の時だけでなく、霧や霧雨、露の時にも見られる。運が良ければ、くっきり見える虹とぼんやりした虹のダブル虹が見られるかもしれない。しかし、本当に触れることは一度もないのだ。

1-4 Cows （牛）
Most people like to drink milk. But have you ever thought about cows, the animals we get our milk from? Cows are interesting animals and, in some ways, similar to humans. According to some scientists, cows are more comfortable when they are with other cows they know, than when they are with cows they don't know. This means that cows have friends, and feel stressed when they are separated from their friends, just like humans.
ほとんどの人は牛乳を飲むのが好きだ。しかし、今まで私たちが牛乳をもらっている動物の牛について考えたことがあるのか。牛は面白い動物で、ある点で人間に似ている。科学者によると、自分たちが知らない牛といる時より、知っている牛と一緒にいる時のほうが安心するという。このことは、牛にも友達がいてその友達と離れてしまうとストレスを感じるということで、まさに人間と同じである。

1-5 The Underwater Waterfall （水中の滝）

Near Mauritius, a country 2000 kilometers off the coast of Africa, there is an underwater waterfall. Of course, it isn't a real underwater waterfall, but an optical illusion. When seen from the air, sand on the ocean floor creates an image that looks like a waterfall. The illusion is caused because Mauritius is still a relatively young island and growing. Sand from the beaches is being washed off the coast and into the deep ocean.

アフリカ沿岸から２０００km離れた国モーリシャスの近くに水中の滝がある。もちろん、本当の水中の滝ではなく、目の錯覚である。上空から見ると、海低の砂が滝のように見える感じを生み出しているのだ。モーリシャスはまだ比較的最近できた島で成長しているので、錯覚が生まれる。砂浜の砂が海岸から流されて、海底深くへ落ちていくのである。

2-1 The Seahorse （タツノオトシゴ）

Have you ever seen a seahorse? It has a long nose, or snout, and the shape of its head makes it look like a horse. When they are swimming, seahorses look clumsy. They steer by using fins behind their eyes. They are the slowest fish in the world! Because they have no teeth, look so delicate, and are poor swimmers, they may seem weak animals. However, because of their excellent camouflage and their ability to move very quietly in the water they are excellent hunters!

タツノオトシゴを見たことがあるだろうか。長い鼻、すなわち突き出た鼻があって、頭は馬みたいにみえる。泳いでいるときは、タツノオトシゴはぎこちなく見える。目の後ろにあるヒレを使い泳ぐ方向をコントロールする。世界一泳ぐのが遅い魚であるのだ！歯が全くなく、華奢な外見、そして泳ぐのが下手なので、弱い動物に見える。しかし、完璧なカモフラージュと、とても静かに泳ぐ能力があるため、素晴らしいハンターなのだ！

2-2 Honesty and Lying （正直と嘘）

We often hear the phrase, "Honesty is the best policy." But not everybody is honest. Do you know when someone is lying? We tend to think people who are lying move a lot. However, many liars don't move at all, or may just give a small smile when speaking. Also, they make more eye contact than usual, because they are trying too hard to appear to be telling the truth. Watch for signs from people around you to see if they are being completely truthful.

「正直は最上の策」ということわざをよく耳にする。しかし、みんなが正直者というわけではない。誰かが嘘をついているとき、あなたはわかるだろうか。嘘をついている人は多動になると考えがちだ。しかし、嘘をついている人の多くが全く動かなかったり、話している時に少し微笑むだけだったりする。また、いつもより人と目を合わせる、なぜなら本当のことを話しているように見せようと必死になっているからだ。周りにいる人が本当のことを言っているかどうか、身振りに気を付けて見てみよう。

2-3 Polar Bears （白熊）

The polar bear is the largest carnivore, or animal that eats meat, that lives on land. Although they look white, their skin is black and their fur is actually clear. Some people say that when polar bears want to hide in the snow, they cover their black noses with their paws. Polar bears are excellent swimmers and can swim for hours on end. They need to live in cold, icy areas to catch their food. However, due to global warming, their habitats are being threatened.

白熊は陸で生活する最も大きい肉食獣、すなわち肉を食べる動物である。白にみえるにも関わらず、肌は黒で毛は透明だ。雪に隠れる時に黒い鼻を手で隠すと言われている。白熊は泳ぐのは得意で数時間休まずに泳ぐこともできる。餌を獲るために寒いところで生活しなければならない。しかし、地球温暖化の影響で生息地がなくなる可能性がある。

2-4 How Long is a Jiffy? （「ジッフィー」ってどれくらいの時間？）

If we go out for a short time, we might say, "I'll be back in a jiffy," to say we will return soon. Most people probably think that a 'jiffy' simply refers to a short amount of time, but in fact it has a true measurement. 'Jiffy' has been used to describe different lengths of time in different fields of science over the past two or three centuries. However, these days, scientists and engineers generally agree that a 'jiffy' is one tenth of a second.

ちょっとだけ出掛ける時に「『ジッフィー』に戻って来る」と言う場合がある。ほとんどの人が「ジッフィー」は「短い時間」という意味と認識しているが、実際に正確な定義はある。科学の異なる分野ではこの２００～３００年間に「ジッフィー」を異なる時間の長さと定義していた。しかし、現在は科学者と技術者の定義は一秒の十分の一であると一致している。

2-5 Shorthand （速記）

Shorthand is an abbreviated form of writing that uses symbols to substitute words. This allows the writer to take notes more quickly than the usual way. There are many forms of shorthand, but the most popular way uses symbols and abbreviations for words and common phrases, which allows someone well-trained in the skill to write just as quickly as people speak. People who are able to write rapidly using shorthand can often find jobs at law courts or government offices to record meetings and conversations.

速記は言葉の代わりに記号を使う、省略した書き方のことで、書く人が普通の書き方よりもっと速くメモが取れるようにしてくれる。速記にはさまざまな方法があるが、一番よくつかわれている方法は、言葉や一般的なフレーズを記号化したり省略したりする方法である。これを極めた人は話す速さと同じくらい速く書くことができる。速記を用いて書くことができる人はよく裁判所や行政機関に勤め先を見つけ、会合や会話のやり取りを記録する。

3-1 Strait of Gibraltar （ジブラルタル海峡）

Between Spain and Morocco, you can find the Strait of Gibraltar. At 14 kilometers, this is the shortest distance between the two continents, Europe and Africa. Many cargo ships travel through the Strait of Gibraltar and there are also regular ferries transporting people between Spain and Morocco. Some people have discussed the possibility of building a bridge between these two countries, and several designs have been proposed by engineers. Although nothing has been finalized, the day when we can easily drive from Africa to Europe in just a few minutes may soon become a reality.

スペインとモロッコの間に、ジブラルタル海峡がみられる。これは二つの大陸、ヨーロッパ大陸とアフリカ大陸間で一番短い距離であり、たった１４kmなのだ。多くの貨物船がジブラルタル海峡を通って航海し、スペインとモロッコ間で人々を乗せている定期フェリーもある。この二か国間で橋を建てられないかと話し合っている人もおり、いくつかのデザインがエンジニアによって設計されている。何も最終決定はなされていないが、アフリカからヨーロッパまでをほんの数分で楽に車で移動できる日が、そう遠くないうちに現実になるかもしれない。

3-2 Japanese Carp （日本の鯉）

The Japanese *koi*, or carp fish, is commonly kept as a pet in Japan. Japanese carp are closely related to goldfish. This is easily noticeable by looking at their orange, white, red, black, and yellow colors. Carp can grow up to one meter long and like to live in water that is about 20 degrees Celsius. Carp eat both plants and animals, consuming other kinds of fish, lettuce and even watermelon. They usually live between 25 and 30 years, but can live much longer. The oldest ever carp, named Hanako, lived well over 200 years!

日本の鯉はコイ科の魚だが、日本では広くペットとして飼われている。日本の鯉は金魚の仲間である。鯉のオレンジや白、赤、黒、そして黄色など見た目からすぐわかるだろう。鯉は１ｍまで成長し、摂氏２０度くらいの水に好んで生息する。鯉は植物と動物、他の種類の魚やレタス、はたまたスイカまでも食べる。たいてい２５年～３０年生きるが、もっとずっと長く生きることもある。今までで一番長寿の鯉は、「花子」という名前で、２００年以上も生きたのだ！

3-3 Central Park （セントラルパーク）

One of the most famous places in New York City is Central Park. Central Park is adorned with greenery, sculptures, fountains, and monuments. The land for Central Park was bought in 1853 for five million dollars, but is now worth 530 billion dollars. Central Park is home to a great variety of animals, 20 parks, baseball fields, outdoor concert theaters, and even a zoo. If you were to walk from one end of Central Park to the other, it'd take you 50 minutes. Central Park is a great place to visit while in New York.

ニューヨーク市でもっとも有名な場所のひとつといえばセントラルパークだ。セントラルパークは緑、彫刻、噴水やモニュメントで彩られている。セントラルパークの土地は１８５３年に５００万ドルで買われたが、現在では５３００億ドルの価値がある。セントラルパークはさまざまな種類の動物、２０もの公園、野球場、屋外コンサート場そして動物園までもがある。セントラルパークの端から端までを歩こうとすれば、５０分はかかるだろう。セントラルパークはニューヨーク滞在中に訪れるにはものすごくいい場所だ。

3-4 Salto Hotel （サルトホテル）

Tequendama Falls in Colombia has always been a popular tourist attraction. To accommodate visitors, Salto Hotel was built in 1928 on the edge of a tall cliff, providing guests with breathtaking views. Unfortunately, the river below the hotel became contaminated, causing the falls to lose their popularity. As a result, Salto Hotel hit hard times, and eventually closed down in the early 1990s. After that, the hotel remained empty, becoming a spooky building that many believed was haunted. Recently, however, Salto Hotel was turned into a museum, returning it to the popularity it once knew.

コロンビアのテケンダマ滝は常に人気の観光スポットである。１９２８年に観光客を泊めるために、サルトホテルは高いがけのふちに建てられ、宿泊客に息をのむ絶景を提供している。残念なことに、ホテルの下にある川が汚染されてしまい、滝への評判が失われる原因になっているのだ。結果として、サルトホテルは苦しい状況に直面し、ついには１９９０年代初頭に閉鎖された。その後、サルトホテルは無人のままで、お化けが出ると多くの人に思われている不気味な建物になりつつある。しかしながら、最近ではサルトホテルは美術館に姿を変え、かつて知れ渡っていた人気を取り戻しつつある。

3-5 Pluto （冥王星）

Pluto was discovered in 1930 and for many years was accepted as the planet furthest from the sun in our solar system even though sometimes, it comes a little closer than the planet Neptune. However, in the year 2006, it was decided that Pluto was too small to be considered a full planet, and was reclassified as a dwarf planet. So just how small is Pluto? It is estimated that its diameter is only about 20 percent of that of Earth, meaning it is smaller than Russia and two thirds the size of our moon.

冥王星は１９３０年に発見され、時々、海王星より少し地球に接近するものの、私たちの太陽系において太陽からもっとも遠い惑星として認められていた。しかし、２００６年、冥王星は完璧な惑星としてはあまりに小さすぎると判断され、準惑星に分類されたのだ。では、冥王星は本当にどれくらい小さいのか。直径は地球の直径の約２０％しかないと推定されており、ロシアより小さく月の３分の２の大きさであるということだ。

4-1 Cotton Candy （綿あめ）

At many festivals around the world, you are likely to find cotton candy. Cotton candy is made of one thing: sugar. Cotton candy is made by melting sugar in a dish shaped like a funnel. The melted sugar escapes through tiny holes in the funnel. The sugar turns into a fine thread as it cools, which you can catch on a stick. This becomes the fluffy cotton candy that we all know. Because cotton candy is made of sugar, it goes without saying that it is bad for your teeth. So it may surprise you to hear that it was actually invented by a dentist.

世界中の祭りで綿あめを見つけることができる。綿あめの材料は一つだけ。それは砂糖だ。綿あめ専用じょうごの中で砂糖を溶かすことで作られている。じょうごにある小さい穴から溶けた砂糖が出てくるが、冷めると細い糸になる。それを棒にからめ取るとみんなの知っているふわふわの綿あめになる。綿あめは砂糖で出来ているので歯に良くないのは当たり前だ。だから、綿あめを発明したのは歯医者だったと聞いたら驚くだろう。

4-2 Message in a Bottle （瓶の中のメッセージ）

When we write messages, we usually know who is going to read them. Sometimes, however, we do not know. One way this can happen is by writing a message, putting it in a bottle, throwing it into the ocean, and then waiting for a reply from whoever finds it. Such messages are written by people wanting to have some fun, people looking for love, or even people lost on deserted islands. If you try putting a message in a bottle, don't expect an immediate reply. The oldest message in a bottle was found in 2015, 108 years after it had been thrown into the ocean.

メッセージを書くときに誰が読むか普通分かるだろう。しかし、誰が読むか分からない時もある。メッセージを書いて、瓶に入れて、海に投げて、そしてそれを見つけた人からの返事を待つというのはひとつの方法。このようなメッセージを書くのは楽しいことをやりたい人や愛を探している人、もしくは無人島にいる人だ。もしあなたがメッセージを瓶に入れることを試しても、返事がすぐに来ることを期待しない方がいい。今まで最も古い瓶の中のメッセージは２０１５年に見つけられた。それが海に投げられたのは１０８年前だった。

4-3 Stamp Collecting （切手収集）

People have been collecting stamps since the first stamp, called the Penny Black, was issued in the United Kingdom in 1840. Stamp collecting is still a very popular hobby today; it is said that there are up to 200 million stamp collectors in the world! Some people may collect stamps simply because they look pretty or have various colorful designs on them. Other people may collect them because of the value and the rarity of the stamps. Usually, stamps don't cost very much. However, some of the rarest stamps, such as a Penny Black which has never been used, can be very expensive to buy.

初の切手であるペニー・ブラックが１８４０年にイギリスで発行されて以降、切手を集め続けている人々がいる。切手収集の趣味は今でも人気である。２億人もの切手コレクターが世界にいる、といわれているのだ！切手が美しくカラフルなデザインだから集めるという人もいる。一方で価値や希少性で切手を集める人もいる。たいてい、切手はそんなに高くない。しかしながら、例えば未使用のペニー・ブラックのような希少性の高い切手はとても高価である。

4-4 The Immortal Jellyfish （不死のクラゲ）

The average life expectancy for humans is 71 years. For hundreds of years, movie makers, scientists, and writers have thought about and examined the possibilities of immortality, or living forever. While, at least for now, it seems impossible for humans to ever be able to achieve this goal, there is one type of jellyfish that, in theory at least, can live forever. This jellyfish is found in temperate to tropical regions in all of the world's oceans. Amazingly, when the jellyfish is sick or old, it's able to change back to an early form and begin to grow once again. Nature can be truly amazing!

人間の平均寿命は７１年。この数百年に渡り、映画監督、科学者、または作家などが、不死、つまり永遠に生きることの可能性について考えてきた。現在、人間にはそれは不可能であろう。だが、理論的に永遠に生きることができるクラゲがいる。このクラゲは温帯から熱帯にかけて世界中の海で見られる。驚くことに、そのクラゲは病気になった時や年を取った時に元の状態に戻ることができ、再び成長することができる。自然って本当に素晴らしいものだ！

4-5 Stock Car Racing （改造車レース）

Stock car racing is a type of car racing that is popular in many countries in the world. In the United States it is the second-most popular TV sport! In these races, the cars look similar to regular cars that we see driving on the road every day. However, the engine and other parts of the car make the cars able to go much faster than regular cars. The racing tracks in stock-car racing events are usually oval, and all the turns are to the left. Because the cars drive so fast, sometimes over 200 miles per hour, it can be a very dangerous sport.

改造車レースは世界各国で人気のカーレースだ。アメリカではテレビのスポーツ番組の中で２番人気なのだ！このレースに使われている車は日頃目にする一般の車とよく似ている。しかし、エンジンやその他のパーツのおかげでとても速く走れる。改造車レース大会の競技用トラックはたいてい楕円形で、きまって左回りだ。車は時速２００マイル以上で走るため、とても危険なスポーツだという。

5-1 City Hall Subway Station （シティホール地下鉄駅）

New York City is full of exciting and wonderful places to visit. Some, like the Statue of Liberty, are known by almost everyone, whereas others, like City Hall Subway Station, are not quite as famous. City Hall Subway Station was built in 1904. Because of its location, a lot of care was taken into making its design as attractive as possible. The station looks beautiful with tall tile arches, brass fixtures, and skylights that run along the entire length of the station. Unfortunately, City Hall Subway Station was closed to the public in 1945 because few people used it, and it was unsafe for new longer trains to use the sharp curve at the station.

ニューヨーク市はわくわくするすてきな観光地でいっぱいだ。その中の自由の女神などは、ほとんどみんなに知られている。一方、例えばシティホール地下鉄駅はそれほど有名ではない。シティホール地下鉄駅は１９０４年に建てられた。この立地もあり、できるだけ魅力的なデザインになるよう多くの配慮がなされた。この駅は背の高いタイルのアーチ、真ちゅうの金具、駅全体に張り巡らされた天窓が美しさをはなっている。シティホール地下鉄駅はほとんどの人が利用しなくなり、新しくできた車体が長い電車がその駅にある急カーブのレールを通るのは危険になったため、残念なことに１９４５年に一般利用されなくなった。

5-2 Kaprosuchus Saharicus （カプロスクス・サハリクス）

Paleontologists are people who study animals, including dinosaurs, that existed millions of years ago. Part of their job is to dig certain areas to search for dinosaur bones. In 2001, an interesting find was made in the Sahara desert, a popular place for paleontologists to work. Skeletons of five creatures that lived at the time of the dinosaurs were discovered. One included an almost perfectly preserved skull of a Kaprosuchus Saharicus, an animal that looked like a crocodile with a strong tail for swimming, but also had long legs allowing it to run across land. With a strong nose and tusks like daggers, this creature meant bad news for anything that got in its way.

古生物学者は動物を研究する人々のことで、何百万年も前に存在していた恐竜も含まれている。仕事の一部には、特定の地域を掘り、恐竜の骨を調査することもある。２００１年にサハラ砂漠で興味深い発見があり、古生物学者が研究する人気の場所となっている。恐竜時代に生息していた５種類の生物の骨格が発見された。そのうちの一つである、カプロスクス・サハリクスの頭蓋骨はほぼ完璧に保存されていた。泳ぐためのワニのような強い尻尾があり、しかしそれだけでなく陸を走り回ることができる長い脚をも持った動物である。強い鼻と短剣のような牙のため、この生物の行く手をはばんだものの全ては消されたと思われる。

5-3 Leonardo da Vinci （レオナルド・ダ・ヴィンチ）

Leonardo da Vinci was a leading artist from Italy born in 1452. He also did a lot of study of the laws of science and nature, which helped his work as a painter, sculptor, and inventor. Leonardo da Vinci was immensely talented, being able to play music, and use both hands naturally. In fact, he could paint with one hand and write with his other hand at the same time. Leonardo was also interested in space, and figured out why we can see the entire moon dimly when it is just a thin crescent. He designed many plans for a variety of inventions such as an armored car, a flying ship, and even floating snowshoes.

レオナルド・ダ・ヴィンチは１４５２年イタリア生まれの一流芸術家だった。科学や自然法則をも研究し、画家、彫刻家そして発明家としての業績の助けとなった。レオナルド・ダ・ヴィンチは非常に才能があり、音楽も演奏できたし、生まれつき両利きだった。実は、片手で絵を描き、同時にもう一方の手で字を書くことができた。レオナルドは宇宙にも興味があり、本当に細い三日月の時であっても月全体がうっすら見えるのはどうしてかを解明したのだ。装甲車や空飛ぶ船、はたまた浮かぶかんじきといったあらゆる発明品を多く設計した。

5-4 Green Tea （緑茶）

Although many people tend to associate green tea with Japan, it actually originated in China. Some historians say that green tea was first grown in China almost 5000 years ago and it was brought to Japan by monks during the eighth century. Green tea is proven to have many health benefits, such as helping weight loss, reducing the risk of heart attack, and keeping you looking young. Although many people prefer coffee to help them wake up in the morning, green tea can still give you a similar jolt, without the high caffeine intake. Green tea can be enjoyed in a variety of ways, including as a hot or cold drink, cake, and ice cream.

多くの人が緑茶といえば日本と連想しがちだが、実は中国発祥である。歴史家の中には緑茶は５０００年前の中国で初めて栽培されたという人もおり、８世紀に僧侶によって日本にもたらされたという。緑茶には健康にいい効果が多くあると証明されており、例えば減量の促進、心臓発作のリスクを軽減、そして見た目の若さを保つといった効果がある。多くの人が朝に目を覚ましてくれるコーヒーを好んで飲んでいるが、緑茶だって近いような活力を与えてくれる、しかも高い濃度のカフェインを摂らずに。緑茶はあらゆる面で楽しめる、例えば、温かい飲み物や冷たい飲み物にしたり、ケーキ、アイスクリームに入れたりして。

5-5 Snow （雪）
American singer Bing Crosby once sang about dreaming of a white Christmas. Obviously, to see a white Christmas, we need to see some snow. However, less than 33 percent of people living on Earth have ever seen snow. Snow is formed when water vapor in the air freezes into ice crystals. Even though these snow crystals appear white, they are actually colorless. Their complex structure absorbs sunlight, which makes snow look white. Even though all snow crystals have six sides, no two of these crystals look exactly alike. Trillions upon trillions of these snow crystals falling and building up is what allows us to enjoy winter through skiing, snowboarding, having snow fights, and building snowmen.

アメリカ人歌手、ビング・クロスビーはかつてホワイトクリスマスを夢見ている歌を歌った。当然、ホワイトクリスマスを見るには、それなりの雪が必要だ。しかし、全世界の人のうち雪を見たことがあるのは３３％に過ぎない。雪は水が蒸発して空気中で凍り、氷の結晶になり形成される。この雪の結晶は白く見えるのに、実は透明なのだ。この複雑な構造が日光を吸収し、雪を白く見せている。雪の結晶すべてが六角形だが、同じ結晶は二つとないのだ。落ちてはつもる、何兆もの雪の結晶のおかげで、私たちはスキー、スノーボード、雪合戦、雪だるまづくりを通して冬を楽しむことができる。

6-1 Professional Video Gamers （プロフェッショナルゲーマー）
For many people, playing video games is a way of relaxing by themselves or with friends. But for some people, gaming is a job! Many years ago, competing at video games meant trying to get the highest score at the local video arcade. Now, professional competitors and teams face each other in organized video game competitions held around the world. The prize is no longer the honor of seeing your name at the top of a video arcade leaderboard, but is now thousands or even millions of dollars paid by famous sponsors. Many of these gamers are employed by one or more of these sponsors and practice by playing the same games for eight or more hours a day in order to become the best.

多くの人は、一人ないし友達とリラックスするためにテレビゲームをやる。しかし、テレビゲームをやることが仕事だという人もいる。数年前には、近所のゲームセンターで最高得点を出そうと競い合うだけだった。今はプロフェッショナルゲーマーが個人やチームで世界各国の大会で競争している。優勝賞品は、自分の名前がゲームセンターの順位表のトップに書いてあるという名誉ではなく、大会を提供した有名な会社からの数千ドル、数百万ドルもの大金である。このようなプロフェッショナルゲーマーは有名なスポンサー企業に採用され、最も強いプレーヤーになるために毎日８時間以上同じゲームを練習している。

6-2 Bubble Wrap （気泡シート）
If you ever need to send someone a parcel with glass, or anything else breakable, it might be a good idea for you to use bubble wrap. Bubble wrap is made by trapping air bubbles between two sheets of plastic. The bubbles of air provide a cushion, protecting products from breaking due to being dropped or bumped. Bubble wrap, however, was first designed to be used as wallpaper. It was not popular and did not make much money. The inventors, however, were not deterred and kept looking for ways to sell their product. Three years later, it was bought by a computer company who used it to protect their computers. From there, bubble wrap became an essential product for millions of people around the world.

ガラス、その他壊れやすいものを誰かに送らなければならないとき、気泡シートを使うのがいいだろう。気泡シートは二枚のプラスチックシートの間に気泡を閉じ込めてできている。気泡がクッションの役割を果たし、落下や衝撃による破損から守る。しかしながら、気泡シートは当初は壁紙として使われるためにデザインされた。人気もなくそんなに儲からなかった。しかし、発明した人たちは、あきらめることなく製品を売る方法を模索していた。３年後、コンピューターを保護するためにコンピューター会社によって買われたのだ。そこから、気泡シートは世界中の何百万もの人々にとってなくてはならない製品へと変化したのだ。

6-3 The Metric System （メートル法）

The Metric System is a standardized set of units for expressing time, length, temperature, and various other quantities. Most countries follow the Metric System, using measurements such as grams for weight and centimeters for length. However, there are still three countries, one of which is the United States, that still use older measurement systems. In the United States, weight is often measured in pounds, with one pound being the equivalent of just over 450 grams. To measure length, inches and yards are used, with one inch being equal to about two and a half centimeters and one yard being about 90 centimeters. These measurements, however, are still sometimes used at places such as golf courses even in countries where the Metric System has been introduced.

メートル法は時間、長さ、温度そしてその他のさまざまな量を表す基本的な単位のセットだ。ほとんどの国がメートル法の規則に従っており、重さにはグラム、長さにはセンチメートルといった測定法を用いている。しかし、いまだに旧式の測定法を用いる国が３か国あり、その中のひとつにアメリカがある。アメリカでは重さはよくポンドで測定されており、１ポンド４５０グラムちょっとに相当する。長さを測るにあたっては、インチとヤードが用いられており、１インチは約２ｃｍ半に、そして１ヤードは約９０ｃｍに相当する。これらの測定法はしかしながらいまだに、メートル法が導入されている国でも、ゴルフコースといった所で時々用いられている。

6-4 Sneezing （くしゃみ）

If I were to have you smell some pepper, there is a good chance you would let out a big sneeze. Although sneezing is an automatic reaction in animals, including humans, we don't sneeze while we are asleep. Sneezing is an important part of staying healthy, as it clears the nose of bacteria and viruses. Scientific research has shown that sneezes travel at over 150 kilometers per hour! Sneezing can be so powerful, that it's possible for you to break a rib while sneezing. Some people try to stop a sneeze by breathing through their mouth or pinching the end of their nose. However, trying to stop a sneeze can be very dangerous as it is possible you could rupture a vein in your nose.

コショウのにおいを嗅がされると大きなくしゃみをする可能性が高い。くしゃみは人間を含め動物の自然な反応であるが、寝ている間はくしゃみをしない。くしゃみは健康を保つ大事な行動であり、鼻からバクテリアやウイルスを一掃するからである。科学の研究ではくしゃみは時速１５０ｋｍ以上の速さであると示されているのだ！くしゃみはとても強力になりうるので、くしゃみの際に肋骨を折る可能性もある。人々の中には口呼吸をして、もしくは鼻をつまんで、くしゃみを止めようとする人もいるが、くしゃみを止めようとするのは鼻の血管が切れる可能性があるのでたいへん危険である。

6-5 Octopuses （タコ）

It is generally agreed upon by scientists all over the world that octopuses are extremely intelligent animals. They have four pairs of arms, three hearts, and are able to release a cloud of black ink, making it easier to escape from attackers. Many octopuses, including the amazing Mimic Octopus, are able to change their color and shape to provide camouflage and even copy the appearance and movement of other animals, making them almost impossible to find in the ocean. Many animals trying to hunt octopuses may swim right by them without even noticing. Although all 300 or so varieties of octopus are venomous, it is only the blue-ringed octopus, found in the Pacific and Indian Oceans, that is known to be deadly to human beings.

世界中の科学者たちによってタコは非常に賢い動物だということがおおむね認められている。４対の足、３つの心臓をもち、攻撃する者から、より簡単に逃げられるように大量の墨を放出することができる。驚くべきミミックオクトパスを始め、多くのタコがカモフラージュするために体の色や形を変え、他の動物の外見や動きをそっくりそのまままねできるため、海の中で見つかるのをほぼ不可能にする。タコを捕まえようとしている動物の多くが気づかずに去っていく。約３００種類の多様なタコのすべてが毒を持つが、太平洋とインド洋で見られるヒョウモンダコだけが人間を死に至らすことが知られている。

List of Vocabulary

Word	Meaning	Level	Word	Meaning	Level
a good chance	可能性が高い	6-4	completely	完全に	2-2
abbreviated	略されている	2-5	complex	複雑な	5-5
absorb	吸収する	5-5	[be] considered ~	～だと思われる	3-5
accommodate	泊めることができる	3-4	consume	食べる	3-2
according to ~	～による	1-4	contaminate	汚染する	3-4
achieve	達成する	4-4	cotton candy	綿あめ	4-1
adorn with ~	～で装飾する	3-3	creature	生き物	5-2
appear ~	～に見える	1-3	crescent	三日月	5-3
arc	弧	1-3	crystal	結晶	5-5
armored	装甲を施した	5-3	cushion	衝撃をやわらげるもの	6-2
associate [A] with [B]	[A]といえば[B]を思い出す	5-4	dagger	短剣	5-2
at least	少なくとも	4-4	deadly	命に関わる	6-5
at the same time	同時に	5-3	delicate	華奢な	2-1
bacteria	細菌	6-4	dentist	歯医者	4-1
billion	10億	3-3	describe	細かく説明する	2-4
brass	真ちゅうの	5-1	deserted island	無人島	4-2
breakable	壊れやすい	6-2	deter	妨げる	6-2
breathtaking	息をのむような	3-4	dew	露	1-3
bubble wrap	気泡シート	6-2	diameter	直径	3-5
bump	ぶつける	6-2	dimly	ぼんやりと	5-3
caffeine	カフェイン	5-4	dinosaur	恐竜	5-2
camouflage	偽装	2-1	discover	発見する	3-5
camouflage	偽装	6-5	dwarf planet	準惑星	3-5
cargo ship	貨物船	3-1	endangered	絶滅寸前の	1-1
carnivore	肉食生物	2-3	engine	エンジン	4-5
carp	鯉	3-2	engineer	技術者	3-1
century	100年間	2-4	entire	全ての	5-1
cliff	崖	3-4	environmental	環境の	1-1
clumsy	不器用な	2-1	equivalent	同等のもの	6-3
coast	海岸	1-5	escape	逃げる	6-5
comfortable	快適	1-4	essential	欠くことができない	6-2

Word	Meaning	Level	Word	Meaning	Level
eventually	結局	3-4	inch	インチ	6-3
examine	調べる	4-4	intake	摂取	5-4
exist	存在する	5-2	intelligent	賢い	6-5
extinct	絶滅した	1-1	invent	発明する	4-1
faint	（色が）薄い	1-3	jellyfish	クラゲ	4-4
fin	ひれ	2-1	jolt	活力	5-4
fine	細い	4-1	keep as a pet	ペットとして飼う	3-2
fixture	設備	5-1	life expectancy	寿命	4-4
float	浮かぶ	5-3	look similar to ~	～に似る	4-5
fluffy	ふわふわしている	4-1	measurement	計測	2-4
fog	霧	1-3	measurement	測定法	6-3
form	形成する	1-3	melt	溶かす	4-1
funky	スタイリッシュな	1-1	metric system	メートル法	6-3
funnel	じょうご	4-1	mimic	擬態する	6-5
fur	柔らかい毛	2-3	mist	霧雨	1-3
global warming	地球温暖化	2-3	monk	僧	5-4
goldfish	金魚	3-2	Neptune	海王星	3-5
habitat	生息地	2-3	noticeable by ~	～で分かる	3-2
[be] haunted	～には幽霊が出る	3-4	obviously	明らかに	5-5
hide	隠れる	2.3	ocean	大洋	4-2
historian	歴史家	5-4	ocean floor	海底	1-5
hit hard times	苦しい状況になる	3-4	on end	連続して	2-3
honor	名誉	6-1	once again	もう一度	4-4
human	人間	6-4	optical illusion	目の錯覚	1-5
hunt	狩る	6-5	originate in ~	～で始まる	5-4
hunter	狩人	2-1	oval	楕円形の	4-5
immediate	すぐの	4-2	paleontologist	古生物学者	5-2
immensely	非常に	5-3	part	部品	4-5
immortal	不死の	4-4	peel	（果物などの）皮	1-2
in a jiffy	すぐに	2-4	pepper	コショウ	6-4
in theory	理論的に	4-4	phrase	ことわざ	2-2

Word	Meaning	Level	Word	Meaning	Level
pinch	つまむ	6-4	sneeze	くしゃみ	6-4
planet	惑星	3-5	snout	突き出た鼻	2-1
Pluto	冥王星	3-5	snowshoe	かんじき	5-3
polar bear	白熊	2-3	solar system	太陽系	3-5
policy	方策	2-2	sponsor	提供者	6-1
pound	ポンド	6-3	spooky	不気味な	3-4
preserve	保存する	5-2	stamp	切手	4-3
propose	提案する	3-1	steer	（船などを）操る	2-1
protect	守る	1-1	stick	棒	4-1
provide	与える	3-4	stock car	改造車	4-5
quantity	数量	6-3	strait	海峡	3-1
rapidly	急速に	2-5	structure	構造	5-5
rarity	珍しさ	4-3	substitute	代わりをする	2-5
reaction	反応	6-4	thread	糸	4-1
reality	現実	3-1	threaten	脅かす	2-3
reclassify	再分類する	3-5	touch	触る	1-3
regular	定期的な	3-1	trillion	一兆	5-5
relatively	比較的	1-5	tropical region	熱帯地域	4-4
research	研究	6-4	turtle	亀	1-1
rib	肋骨	6-4	tusk	牙	5-2
rupture	破裂する	6-4	underwater	水中	1-5
sculptor	彫刻家	5-3	unfortunately	残念ながら	3-4
seahorse	タツノオトシゴ	2-1	value	価値	4-3
separate	別れる	1-4	vapor	蒸気	5-5
sharp curve	急カーブ	5-1	vein	血管	6-4
shorthand	速記	2-5	venomous	有毒な	6-5
similar to ~	~に似る	1-4	video arcade	ゲームセンター	6-1
skeleton	骨格	5-2	virus	ウイルス	6-4
skull	頭骸骨	5-2	wallpaper	壁紙	6-2
skylight	天窓	5-1	well-trained	よく訓練されている	2-5
snack	軽食	1-2	yard	ヤード	6-3

[著者紹介]

Adrian Leis（リース　エイドリアン）
宮城教育大学准教授。
オーストラリア出身。1997年に来日後、英会話学校、ALT、私立中学校高等学校の教諭（副担任も含む）を経て、現職に至る。2016年に東北大学大学院博士課程を修了し、現在は英語教育、動機づけ、反転学習を中心に研究を行っている。

Simon Cooke（クック　サイモン）
東北工業大学准教授。
イギリス出身。1996年に来日後、ALT、高等学校での勤務を経て、現職に至る。現在は英語教育、動機づけを中心に研究を行っている。

無敵リスニング〈上級〉
Ultimate Listening〈Advanced〉

著　者	Adrian Leis・Simon Cooke
発行者	武村哲司
印刷所	萩原印刷株式会社

2017年3月25日　第1版第1刷発行
2019年3月5日　第2版第1刷発行
2020年9月10日　　第2刷発行

発行所　株式会社 開拓社

〒113-0023 東京都文京区向丘1丁目5番2号
電話（03）5842-8900（代表）
振替 00160-8-39587
http://www.kaitakusha.co.jp

© 2019 Adrian Leis and Simon Cooke　　ISBN978-4-7589-2311-8 C0082

JCOPY〈出版者著作権管理機構　委託出版物〉
本書の無断複製は著作権法上での例外を除き禁じられています。複製される場合は、そのつど事前に、出版者著作権管理機構（電話 03-5244-5088、FAX 03-5244-5089、e-mail: info@jcopy.or.jp）の許諾を得てください。